Palm Reading
for Everyone

An Earth Lodge Guide to Easy Hand Analysis

By Sandra Cointreau

An Earth Lodge® Publication
http://www.earthlodgebooks.com
Roxbury, Connecticut

This work is dedicated to my daughter,
whose talents, skills, and courage continue to
inspire me and whose love fills my heart.

CONTENTS

1   Why do We Read Palms?   1

2   The Initial Scan of the Two Hands – Flexibility, Muscle,   7
     Texture and Size

3   The In-Depth Study of the Palm – Finger, Palm and Nail   10
     Shapes; Major Lines; Minor Lines; Marks; and Mounts

4   Printing the Palm – Ink Print, Photograph   59

5   References   61

6   Work Sheet for Palm Reading Observations   62

     Acknowledgements   67

     About the Author   68

1

WHY DO WE READ PALMS?

Do you notice the body language of your friends, as they hunch their shoulders or cross their arms or clench their fists? Do you notice the facial expressions of the people around you, as they look away and downward, or grimace, or tighten their jaw? Do you notice the expressive movement of their hands and arms as they emphasize what they are saying in openness and joy? And your animals...do you notice when they stand on their toes and are rigid in posture, versus bending their knees softly, sink down into their heels, and bow their head?

Do you notice the pitch and frequency of sounds made by your horses or dogs and what these different sounds mean? Do you notice the high alarm call of the lead herd mare or stallion, versus the low nickering of a mother to its foal, and how one sound carries far and the other is only for close proximity. Have you seen that pitch and frequency/speed of sounds with people could be comparable in conveying emotion?

Palmistry is another tool in our ability to understand those around us and be aware of what is happening in their lives. The palm influences the person's view of themselves, and the palm reflects the person's use of their hands.

As with each animal that comes into this world, each person comes in with a unique personality that manifests in the early weeks. Experience and decisions alter that personality somewhat, but we are who we are at the core, from the beginning of each life.

As a breeder of standard poodles for 20 years, I have an outside professional test each puppy at age 7 weeks for personality, focus for training, connection to people and interest in various types of work. As I follow the lives of these pups over the next 10-15 years, through their families and among my own breeding group, I am amazed at how true to their early testing outcomes they all remain. I've seen that an alpha dog arrives as an alpha dog, and the same is true with the alpha mare of the herd of female horses. Humans have some of that initial baseline presented in their arrival palms, as the path the soul intends as its basic attributes and characteristics in this life.

Scientists have confirmed that animals and people have genetic memories from all their ancestors. After all, DNA is passed live from parents to newborns through their live sperms and eggs, so any memories embraced in our DNA coding is passed on. How else can each bird species have an entirely different way to make a nest and to migrate or overwinter? How else does each new animal, even if separated from its parents at birth, know what and how to safely eat and drink? Doesn't it make sense that some of our memory even relates to our memories of hands our ancestors have seen and studied over time?

The Basis for this Book

I'm writing this book to try to simplify and clarify palmistry. There are in-depth books available with many photos of client hands and related discussions. But, I haven't found a straight-forward quick reference of the major features of the hand. I'm hoping this book provides that for you.

I'm an engineer by profession and have an analytical and research oriented approach to everything that I do. At the same time, I have been a painter all my adult life and embrace the non-analytical side of life. My engineering work has taken me to more than 60 countries. In many, I have met palm readers and learned from them. Many have a purely psychic intuitive approach, where the hand they view triggers their intuition.

My own approach is first analytical, and then after analysis I settle myself into a semi-meditative state and allow the intuitive to come through. While the focus of this book is analytical, there is no denying that every element of assessing palms involves some intuitive element. As we slowly examine the hands in a step-by-step process, we can enter into a semi-meditative state that allows our higher self to inform us. Take the time to allow this connection to your higher self. Be patient until there is clarity. Trust your intuition, as it comes from your source, your soul.

This material is based on my experience since the early 1980s in palm reading, which included basic teachings from in-depth original texts that form the foundation for palmistry today, especially the Cheiro and Benham books. It is comprehensive of the main elements and enough information to do palm reading.

For the fine points and unusual markings, the detailed reference books are from masters who show photos of many hands and their special features, so that the more complicated assessments can be made. I find the Cheiro and Benham books to be excellent and rich in detail, even though they are not easy to use. They are referenced at the end of this book for the most serious palmist students.

Each hand and palm is unique. Large or small, round or square, smooth or course, pink or pale, flexible or inflexible? While assessing each part of the hand and line of the palm, analytical determinations need to be made. But, not all features are entirely clear, and that is where intuition is needed. With experience, it will become easier to decide how best to characterize the palms you are viewing, using both your analytical and intuitive ability.

This book is enough to enable you to do basic and comprehensive readings and develop your skills through experience and the many affirmations you will receive from the people whose hands you read. Be easy and relaxed and let the readings come through with a sense of fun and faith

Is Palmistry a Window into Who We Are?

All hands change over time. So nothing in a palm reading is a forever forecast. A palm reading is a snapshot in time of all that has happened over each life until that moment.

Our hands influence how we see ourselves. They present a mirror, indicating all through the day, our characteristics, strengths and weaknesses. We see more of our hands all day than we see of any other part of our body. We become our hands...and our hands become us.

The two hands start out with certain lines, mounts and shapes indicating the fate that is the baseline. As each person works, plays, loves and uses their hands, these features may change a little, or alot.

We use both hands. In some people, one hand is very dominant. In other people, the difference between the hands is less pronounced. The palmistry client should indicate which hand they most comfortably use, rather than which hand they may have been required to use during childhood training.

Because of its use, the dominant hand is the primary hand to change because it is the most active in your life activities. Therefore, the non-dominant hand holds most features of the baseline, and the dominant hand shows what you have done with the baseline.

The non-dominant hand thus presents the baseline. It is the starting point, like a potential map with strengths and weaknesses to be altered as we move along our path. The starting baseline was determined by our soul, in its time between lives. It reflects anticipated challenges and lessons that we would work on in this life.

Our baseline is our opening paragraph to the chapter of our life book. It is the baseline depicting the foundation of our soul evolution in this life. As we experience spiritual unfoldment, as we move along our path of lives to strive to become a "non-returner", we experience challenges, opportunities, and growth. Ideally, each life will progressively lead us to nirvana, a status where we do not have to return to the physical realm for more lessons. A non-returner is a "buddha". Some non-returners come back to teach and lead us as prophets, even though they don't need to return.

 Just as the soul chooses its parents, as part of its baseline for this life, other starting conditions of temperament, health, and settings are chosen by the soul on entry to this incarnation. All of these are reflected in the hand that is minimally used, and in the dominant hand when we are a young child.

These baseline hand conditions are reflected in the flexibility, muscle, texture, shape, size, lines, mounts, and marks of the hand. Despite what we have been given at the start, there is always free choice and the opportunity to constantly adapt, change, and grow. A short life line doesn't have to remain a short life line. A hand without any marriages doesn't have to remain a hand without marriages.

2

THE INITIAL SCAN OF
THE TWO HANDS

How Do We Start?

The first step in reading the palms is to look at both hands. Look at the front and the back of each hand and take your time. Turn the hands back and forth, examine their color, size, flexibility and openness. Notice if the client keeps their hands open for you, or holds them closed between your examinations that open them. Notice if the client is comfortable or uncomfortable with having their hands examined and touched.

After the initial examination where you focus on the big picture of the two hands, ask the person which hand is most dominant. Then hold the two palms up in front of you and look at them together to see if you see any major differences between the two. Are there major differences in their shape, color, openness, complexity of lines, length of lines and fullness of mounds.

What follows are the main features to examine when looking at both hands.

Flexibility

Bend the hands (held out closed and flat) with pressure to measure flexibility.

By bending the fingers backward, flexibility is determined. A very flexible hand bends back nearly 90 degrees with minimum pressure. A moderately flexible hand bends back in an arc about 30 to 45 degrees. A stiff hand is not flexible to be bent backward and may not even be able to be straight.

- High flexibility indicates highly impressionable person. If the thumb also bends back easily, it indicates generosity. Flexible people may have spending problems.
- A moderately flexible hand is versatile, intuitive and open-minded. Can be impressionable, but not as much as a highly flexible hand.
- A firm hand indicates vital force, but also being careful with feelings and not revealing or impulsive.
- A stiff hand is extremely rigid, indicating cautious, responsible, hard working person.

Muscle

Touch the hands under pressure to assess muscle:

- A flabby hand has flesh easily crushed together when squeezed gently. Indicates low physical energy, and person who may dislike exertion of any type. If flabby and thick, may indicate over-indulgence of any type. If flabby and thin, indicates weakness and low energy level.
- A soft hand has lack of boney feeling under pressure, but more energy than the flabby handed person.
- An elastic hand springs back, not easy to crush. An elastic handed person shows vitality, adaptability, action. Adaptable to new ideas and conditions.

- A firm hand is slightly elastic. Firm handed person is adaptable, but not as much as the elastic handed person.
- A hard hand does not yield under pressure. Mostly found on men. A hard handed person lacks flexibility and holds in their energy. May be subject to temper and stress diseases.

Texture

Feel and see the texture of the skin. Skin texture is an indicator of the use of the hands, as described below:
- Soft and fine skin indicates easily likely to be physically or emotionally sensitive.
- Hard and coarse skin indicates detachment from physical and emotional sensitivity. The harder the skin, the more likely the person needs to be physically active and to spend time outside to release physical energy.
- Medium skin indicates a balance of sensitivity and practical behavior.
- Many fine lines that are not the palmistry lines indicate nervousness and sensitivity. These fine lines are the same color as the background skin and are not marks or lines of influence. If only on certain parts of the hand, the fine lines may indicate sensitivity only in the issues associated with that part of the hand.

Size

Size is relative to age, gender, and body size. Examine the hand in the context of the person:
- Large hands tend to gravitate toward small things, details.
- Small hands tend to notice the big picture.
- Narrow hands tend to reveal a narrow perspective on life, especially if stiff and hard.

3

THE IN-DEPTH STUDY OF THE PALM

From this point forward, most of your work in palm reading the person's hands will be focused on the dominant hand. You will go through the steps in the sections below to closely examine the dominant hand. Your thoughts can be noted in the worksheet at the end of this book. I copy this worksheet and give my notes to the person at the end of the reading.

After you are through with your careful reading of the dominant hand, you may return to the non-dominant hand to see if there are important palmistry changes that have occurred in the person's life from the baseline hand that is non-dominant. It may lead you to indicate to the person that they have done things to improve their palm from what they were given as a baseline. In some cases, it may lead you to suggest that they need to work on their health or on other issues, as they have more potential than is reflected in the dominant hand.

Each palmist develops their own step-by-step process. I like to proceed through the following steps, working from the large contextual features of hand and finger shape, then moving to the smaller focused features of mounts, lines and marks.

Hand Shape

The shape of the hand is a primary indicator of character to note. There are four basic hand shapes:

- Square palm hands (earth hand) often have matching short square fingers. The Square palm person is methodical, reliable, physical, nature loving, and makes decisions cautiously and logically. Negatives: May be critical and suspicious.
- Round palm hands (fire hand) often have matching short rounded fingers. The Round hand person is warm, sociable, artistic, creative. Negatives: May be impulsive, not finish things, egocentric.
- Rectangular palm hands (philosophical hand) often have fingers that are long and knotty. The rectangular palm hand has logic, diplomacy, and is kindhearted and quick-minded. Negatives: May be a perfectionist and tedious.
- Narrow palm hand (air or psychic hand) often have fingers that are long and tapered at the ends. The narrow palm hand person is contemplative, intuitive, visionary, idealistic, poetic, spiritual. Negatives: May be nervous, overly sensitive, out of touch with reality.

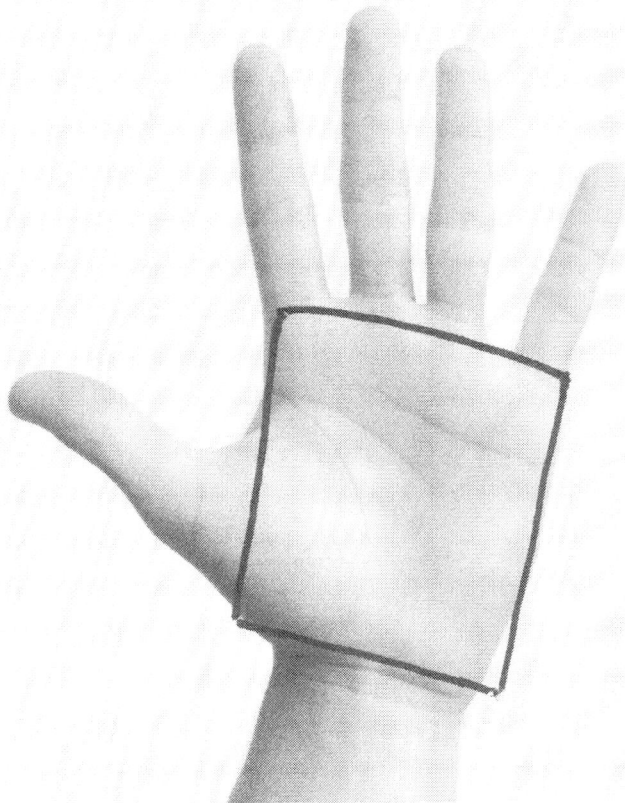

round
fire

narrow
water

rectangle
air

square
earth

Finger Shape and Angle

The fingers are designated with the named for mythological gods, and they represent characteristics of those gods. They are named as follows:

- 1st finger – Jupiter indicates leadership, protection, and religion characteristics.
- 2nd finger – Saturn indicates responsibility and service characteristics.
- 3rd finger – Uranus indicates sociability and security characteristics.
- 4th finger – Mercury indicates communication and flexibility characteristics.

Finger and hand shape are the main indicators of mental quality; and it is the mental quality that most affects any aspect of the hand.

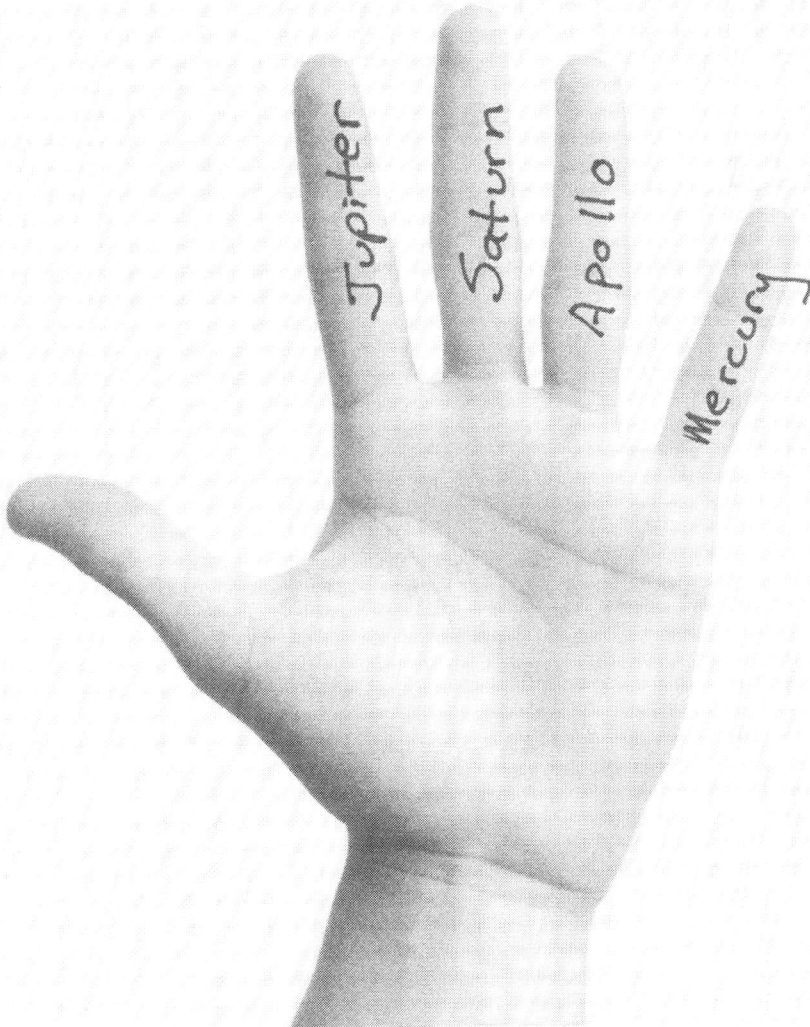

Smooth or Knotted

Fingers are firstly assessed as either smooth or knotted. Smooth fingers are fairly common. Knotty fingers (unless due to arthritis) indicate a person with a strong analytical mind, tending to research deeply into issues. They tend not to be emotionally expressive.

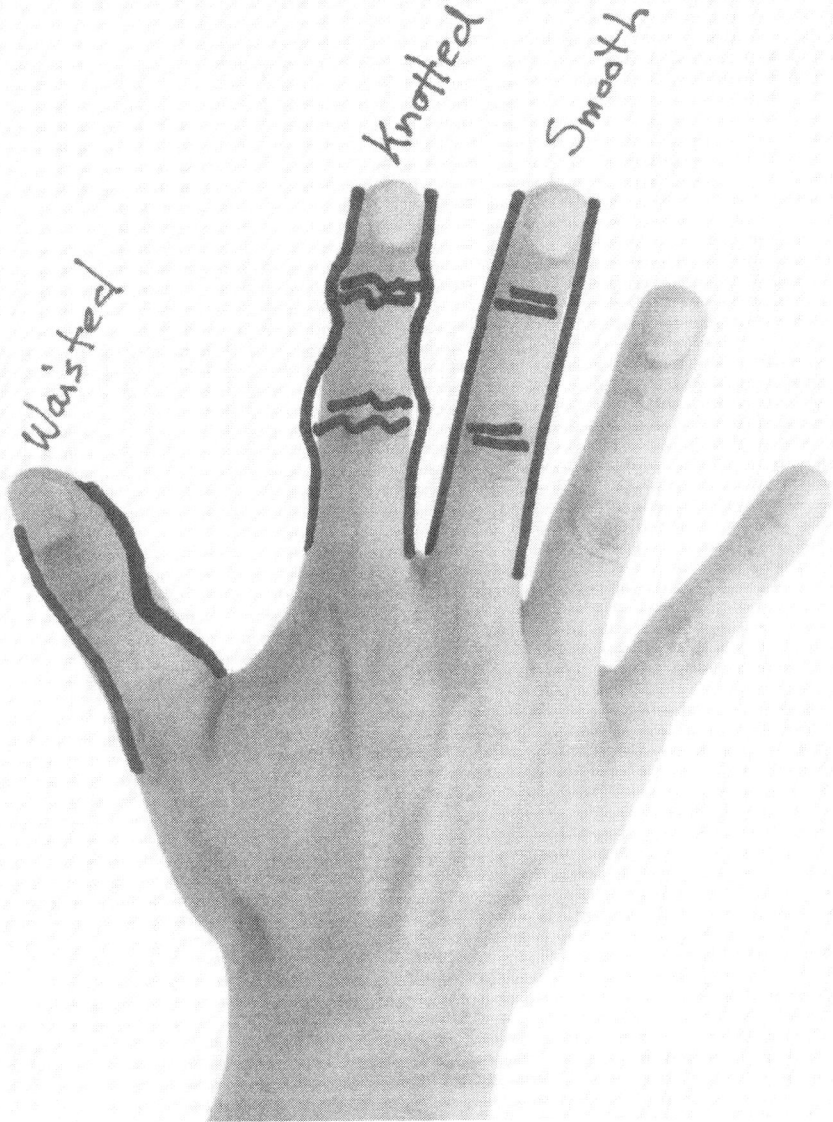

Phalanges

There are three phalanges. If any is longer than the others, it indicates stronger emphasis on that phalange, as described below.

- From top to bottom, the finger phalanges represent mental order, practical order, and material order.
- From top to bottom, the thumb phalanges from tip to bottom represent will, logic, and the mount of Venus.

Most commonly, finger phalanges tend to be the same width. When the base phalange of the fingers is thick and puffy, compared to the other phalanges, the subject may consider their own comfort before that of others.

When the end of the thumb has a bulbous top phalange, a tendency toward stubbornness and repressed anger could be indicated, especially if the tip also angles backward. While outbursts are possible, this trait can be positively channeled into sports or other competitive endeavors.

Width

Fingers that are narrow indicate a quiet person of low physical energy. These people will generally acquiesce or seek a harmonious agreement, rather than argue or compete. While not physically robust, they may have strong metal or emotional energy to persevere for the long haul. Like a narrow tree that bends in the breeze but readily withstands the storm. On the other hand, a wide finger shows vitality and physical energy. Such a person may be gregarious and sociable.

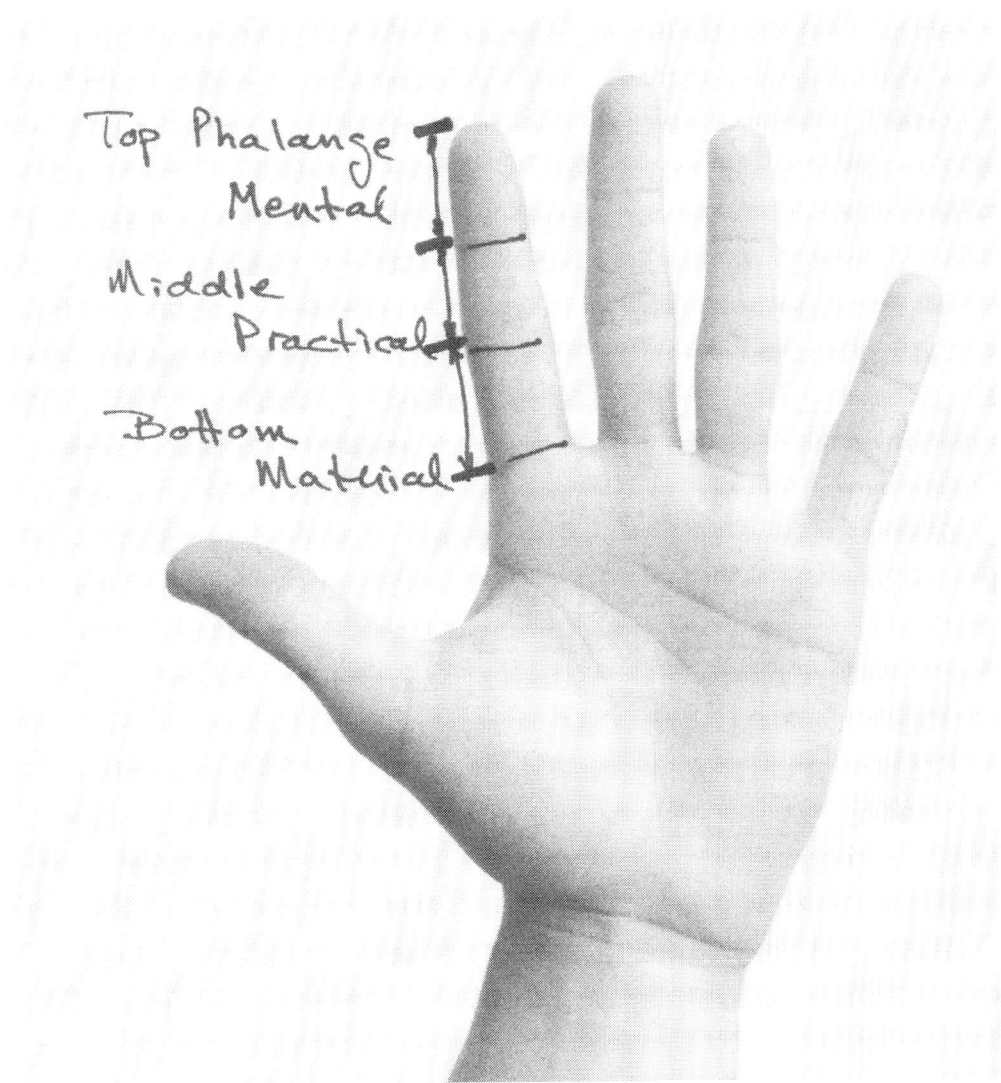

Top Phalange
Mental

Middle
Practical

Bottom
Material

Spread and Angle

Spacing and angles of the fingers when the hand is opened by the client indicate their degree of security. When the fingers are spread wide, the person is generally confident and open. When the fingers are closed, especially when closed and cupped, the person is not confident nor open. Closed fingers indicate difficulty to have trust in people and situations, which is fundamental to enjoying life.

A wide space between only the 1st and 2nd finger indicates independence of thought. Normal spacing between these fingers is between 45-60 degrees angle. As the spacing tends toward 90 degrees, high independence is indicated. Generosity is also indicated with a very high spacing. On the other hand, a hidden thumb inside the palm shows anxiety and insecurity.

A wide space between the 3rd and 4th fingers (Uranus and Mercury) indicates independence of action. When the client consistently returns their hand to a closed position after you have opened it to examine the palm, it indicates a closed personality.

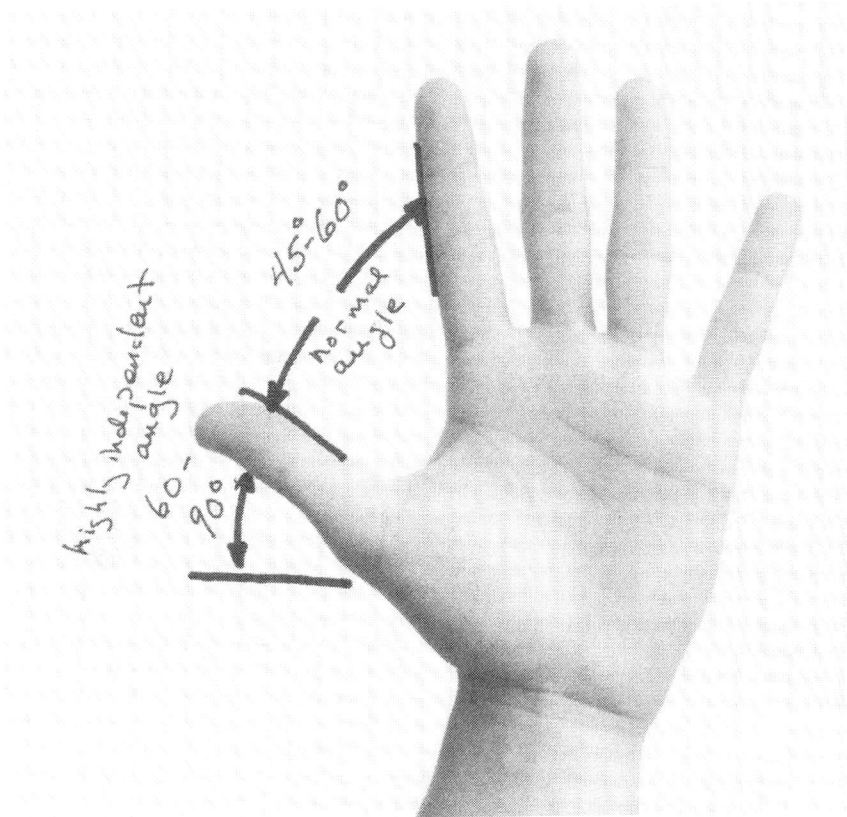

highly independent angle
60-90°

45-60°

normal angle

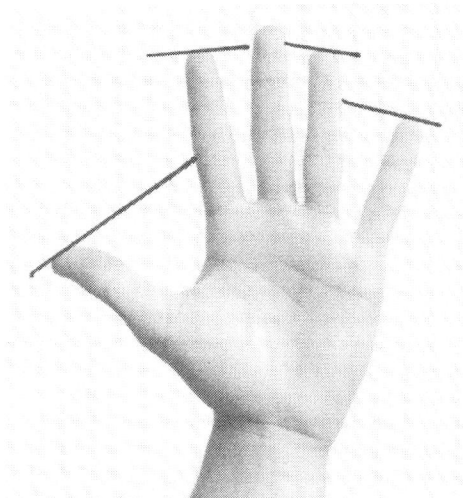

Length

Length of the fingers needs to be considered relative to the length of the palm, as measured from the wrist to the base of the 1st finger (Jupiter). Normally, the palm should be slightly longer than the fingers (up to ½ inch longer). If more than this, then the fingers are considered long. If shorter than the palm, then the fingers are considered short. They indicate the following:
- Long fingers like to plan and analyze. They seek order. They are good at detail.
- Short fingers like to act more spontaneously. They are good at the big picture and having oversight.

A thumb with a long length indicates a person of great will and determination to achieve goals. To be considered long, a thumb would need to reach the knuckle of the 1st finger (Jupiter). If the thumb does not reach beyond the base of the 1st finger (Jupiter) would be considered short. A short thumb would indicate a more emotional intuitive person.

Arch of the Base

Fingers normally are mounted in a relatively straight line across the top of the hand and spaced evenly. Any finger set higher indicates that the importance of that finger is significant. A lower set finger would indicate less importance to that finger. A low set 4th finger (Mercury) would indicate difficulties in communication, which could mean intimacy problems.

Nails

Nails are usually shaped similarly to the fingers. There are many nail features that give information, but most of this information is related to current short-term health, and isn't necessary for a palm reading.

Noting significant unusual color, ridges, flaking, bumps, etc., on nails might warrant comment to the client to monitor for health issues. This is especially valid if supported by health issues noted in the Life Line and Health Line, and their corresponding Marks and Mounts.

Shape

The four basic finger and nail shapes are:
- Rounded fingers and nails indicate a moderate person between intuitive and analytical, balanced between the conic and square fingers and nails.
- Conic fingers and nails indicate a warm friendly person with artistic energy. When the conic finger and nail is particularly pointed, it may indicate a dreamer or psychic nature and difficulty to be grounded in the world
- Square fingers and nails indicate a rational, orderly person with linear thinking and good organizational skills.
- Spatulate fingers and nails indicate an energetic person with an inquiring mind, multiple interests and self-confidence, possibly with scattered energies.

Length

The length of the nail refers only to the base of the nail to its top connection to the finger. The additional length grown beyond the top is not relevant to palmistry. Various lengths provide the following indications:

- Long nails indicate a person who wants harmony and perfection in their life, and is likely gentle diplomatic.
- Short nails indicate a person who is determined and strong, and may be blunt and competitive.

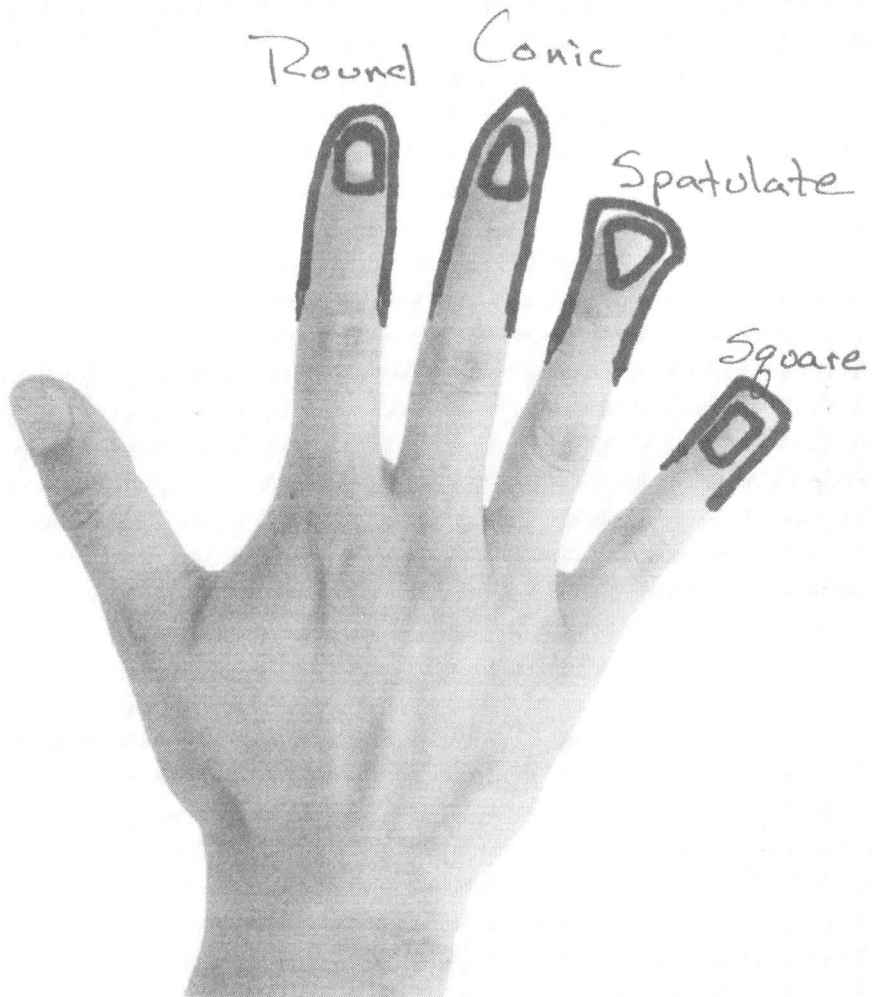

Round   Conic

Spatulate

Square

Mounts:

Mounts are the fleshy bumps on the palm, and the more filled and emphasized they are, the more those mounts have strength and prominence in the personality.

If there are reinforcing Marks, such as vertical lines on Mount, this strengthens the Mount.

Some Mounts are associated with Fingers having the same planetary designation. The first 5 Mounts listed below are associated with fingers. The others are not.

Jupiter Mount (1st finger of same name):
- Has the characteristics of Jupiter or Zeus, the King of Gods.
- Reflects leadership, self-confidence, executive skill, ambition.
- Indicates generosity, extroverted charisma, being gregarious.

Saturn Mount (2nd finger of same name):
- Has the characteristics of the God of judgment.
- Reflects responsibility, careful analysis and decision-making, thoughtful introspection, careful self-preservation, independence.
- Indicates reliability, constancy, guiding principles, prudence, emotional balance.

Apollo Mount (3rd finger of same name):
- Has the characteristics of the God of power and self-expression.
- Reflects education, scholarship, research, artistic effort, creativity.
- Indicates love of beauty, music, intellectual concepts, and likelihood of taking care of appearance.

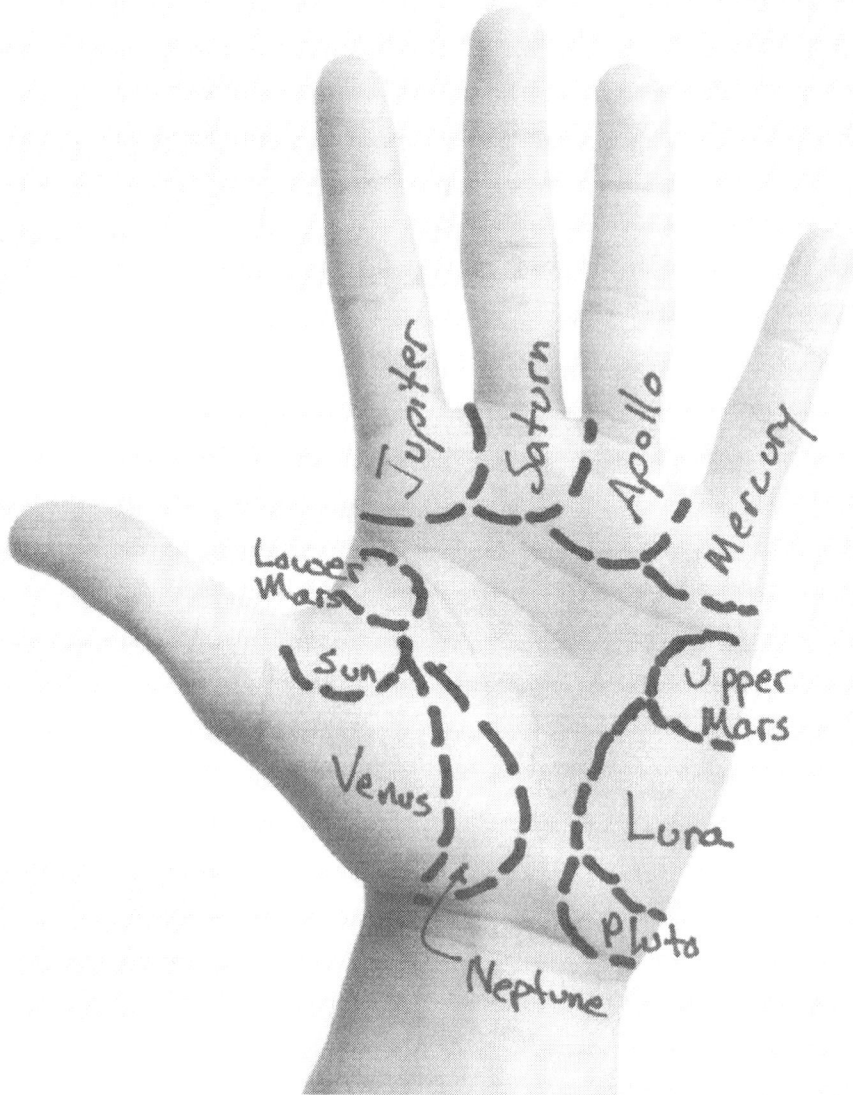

Mercury Mount (4th finger of same name – the little finger):

Mercury Mount (4th finger of same name – the little finger):
- Has the characteristics of the Messenger of the Gods.
- Reflects communication by word and manner, diplomacy, negotiation.
- Indicates love of writing, expression, public speaking.

Venus Mount (thumb):
- Has the characteristics of the Goddess of Love. Considered the most important Mount and Finger, as it can modify all other information revealed by Mounts and Fingers. Its wide arc takes up almost a third of the palm area.
- A good Venus Mount should be higher than the other mounts and smooth and firm to the touch. Ideally, it should also be slightly pink in color.
- Indicates warmth, vitality, energy, and love of life.
- A well-formed Venus Mount strengthens the Life Line.

Upper Mars Mount:
- Has the characteristics of the God of War.
- The Mars Mount is located just below the Mercury Mount (below the 4th finger).
- Indicates courage, determination, valor, ability to overcome obstacles.

Lower Mars Mount:
- On the opposite side of the palm, indicates stronger tendencies to the Upper Mars Mount. Such as stronger courage, determination, and self-determination.

Luna Mount:
- Has the characteristics of the Moon.
- The Luna Mount is located on the palm side that is opposite to the Thumb and Venus Mount.

- Indicates interest in spiritual/religious/sacred pursuits, and abilities of intuition, clairvoyance, clairaudience, prophesy, imagination. Can indicate a nurturing, care-giver nature. Can support artistic endeavors.

Lines

Lines are very different on the "given" baseline hand versus the "evolved" dominant-use hand. Lines change based on our choices and experiences.

Hand and finger shape may not show much change over time. On the other hand, lines, mounts and marks show the greatest potential for change. It is important not to be predictive of outcomes based on the lines, mounts and marks.

Lines that are deep, long, strong in color, and continuous are generally considered positive. Weak thin and short lines, without color depth, and with discontinuities show potential problems in past, as well as problems that occurred in the future.

Marks may be on lines and mend a line, parallel shorter lines may strengthen a line. Crossing lines or other marks may weaken a line. Marks are discussed separately below.

Life Line

- The life line should be curved in a wide arc around the Venus Mount, and not moving past the Fate Line or center of the palm, indicating a warm and responsive life force. It curved line should not hug close to the thumb, which would indicate an inhibited cold life force.
- A branch leaving the life line and moving up towards the 1st finger (Jupiter) indicates optimism in life, and the drive and energy to manifest and overcome.
- Connection of the life line to the head line, and for the length of the connection, indicates dependence on family and lack of independence.
- The life line indicates strength, health, vigor and is the most important line. With discontinuities, it may show problems in the past and possible problems for the future, such as disease and even potential death . But, it is a fully changeable line – like all the lines.

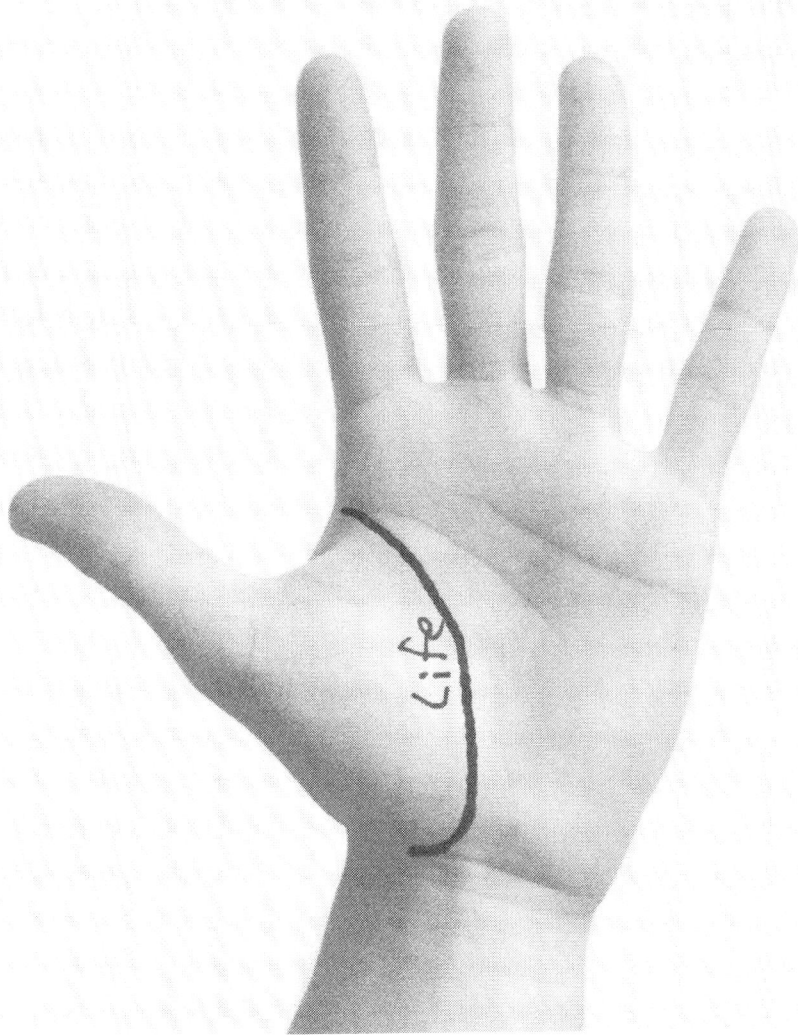

Head Line

- The Head Line indicates mental strength, the ability to be focused on mental work, and psychological disposition.
- Ideally the Head Line is long and curves downward toward the Lunar Mount, which is the area for intuition.
- Small forks at the end indicate balance of realism and imagination, analysis and intuition.
- The greater the angle of the drop of the line toward the Lunar Mount, and the further the distance into the Lunar Mount, is indicative of imagination, creativity and intuition.
- Very straight lines that don't curve downward indicate a primarily analytical, logical mind that is rooted in reality and practicality.
- Short lines indicate limited intellectual interest.

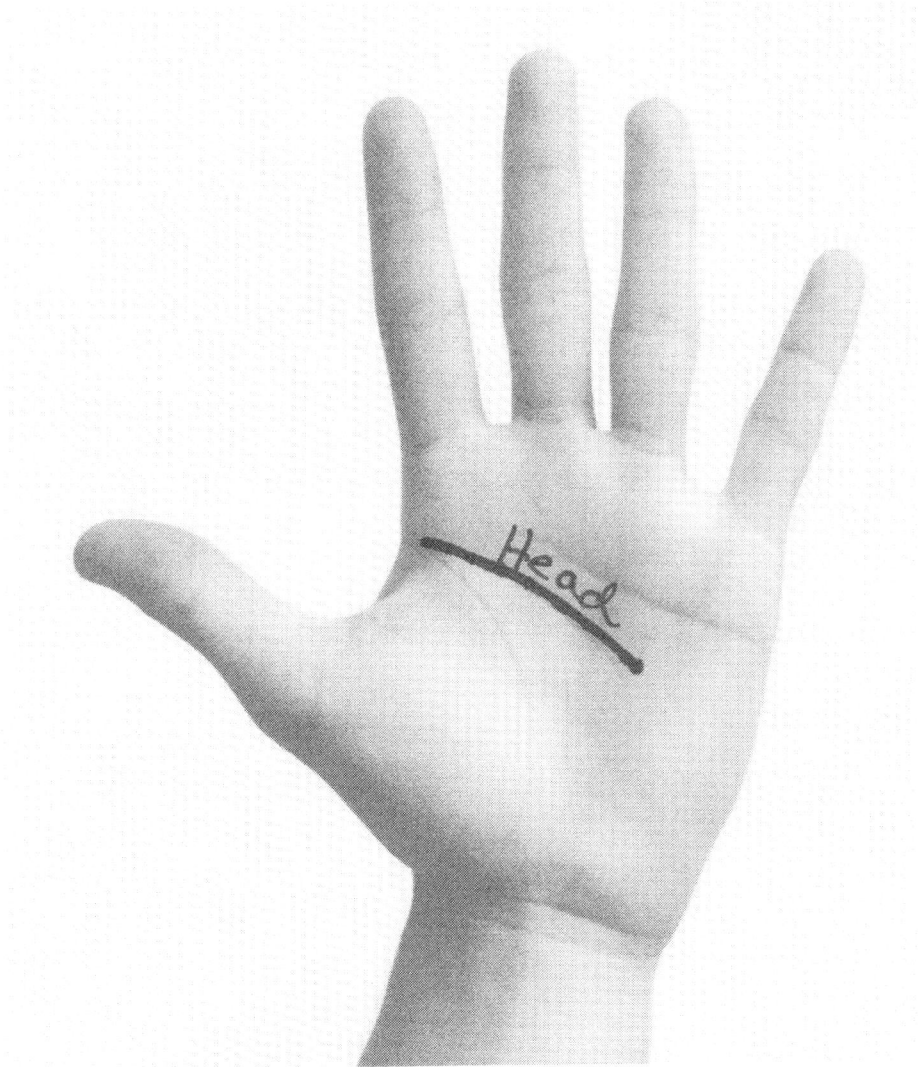

Heart Line

- The Heart Line is the emotional indicator, showing the tendency toward sensitivity, compassion and the ability to have relationships. Ideally, it would curve upward toward the space between the 1st and 2nd fingers. Branches at the end indicate emotional balance.
- When the Head Line and Heart Line are one line, it is called the Simian line, and may indicate emotional extremes. In people with this line, there could be strong capacity to achieve. But, there could be a personality down-side of violence or unpredictable behavior. Studying the whole hand will help to indicate the tendencies, but be careful in this analysis, as the person may be intense to deal with.

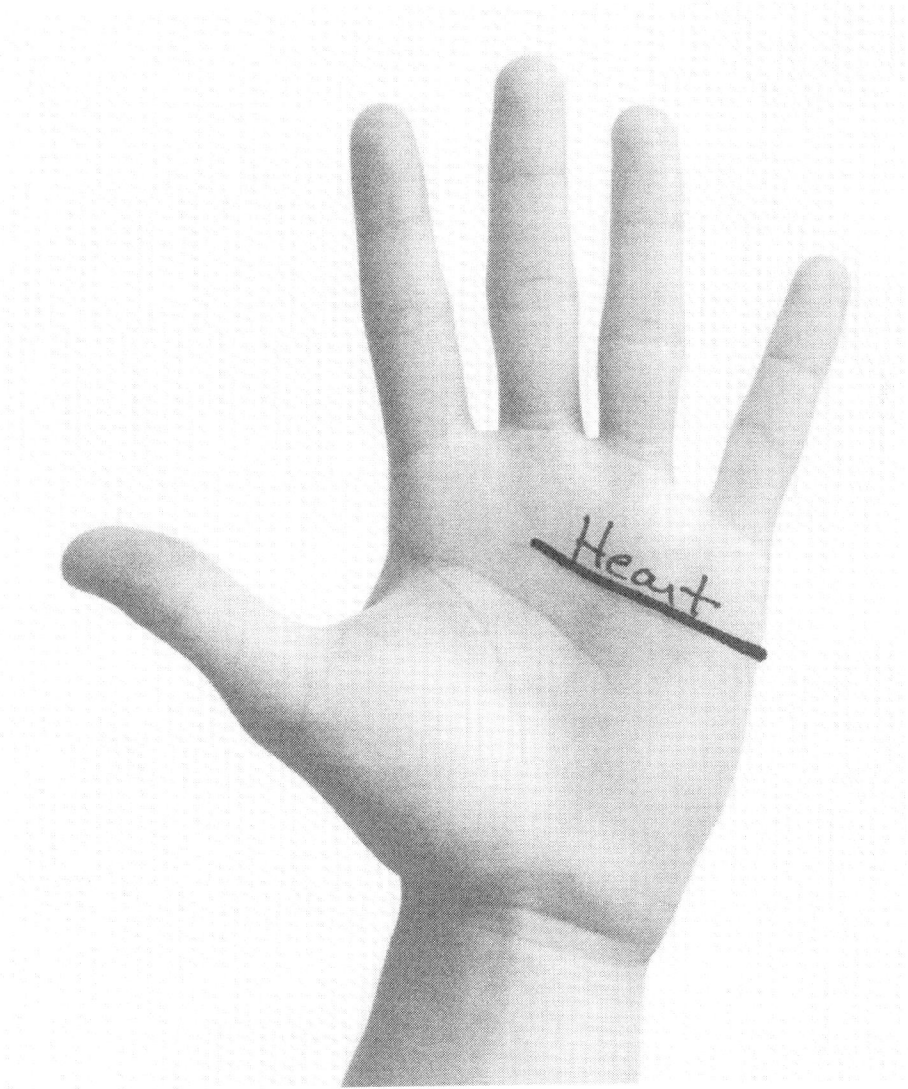

Fate Line

- The fate line (also known as the Line of Saturn) moves upward from above the wrist towards the Saturn Mount.
- The Fate Line indicates destiny, career, achievement, a focused endeavor of some kind. Normally, it does not indicate family as an endeavor, instead indicating an "external" endeavor to caring for family. Family matters are more indicated by the Heart Line.

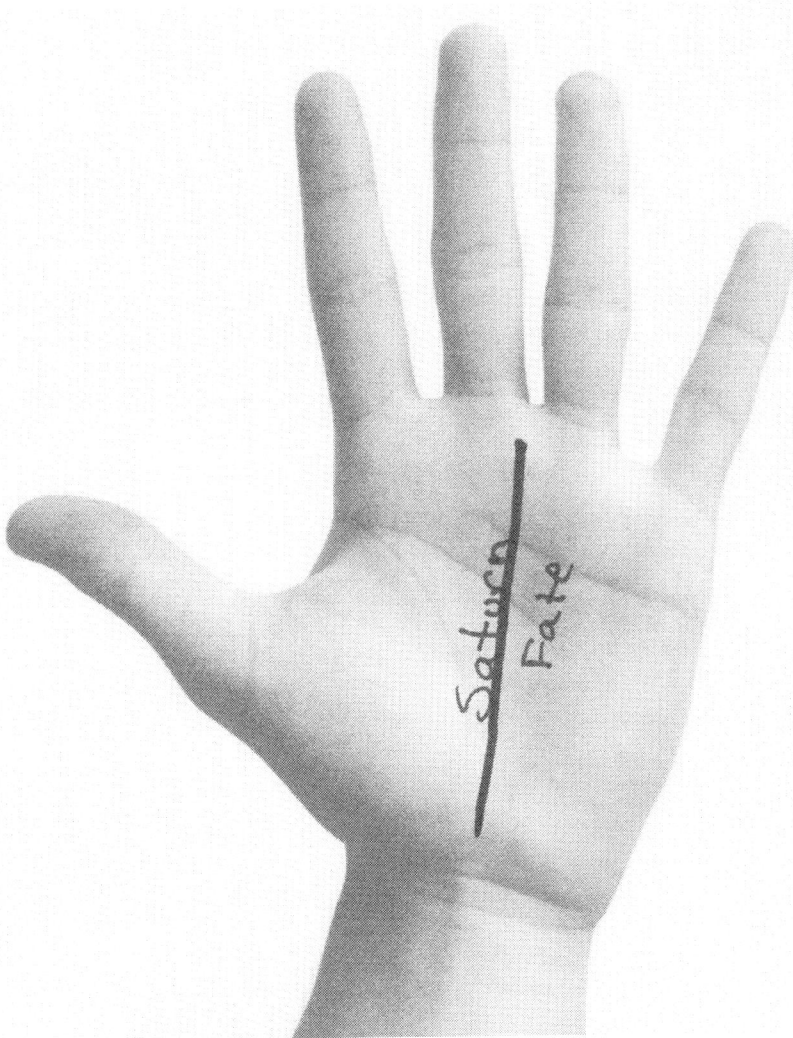

Saturn Fate

Line of Capability

- When it appears, which is not often, the Line of Capability (also known as the Line of Apollo) is found dropping downward from the Mount of Apollo and somewhat parallel to the Line of Fate.
- It indicates honors, success, recognition, rewards and special brilliance in one's endeavors. Often found on successful artists, musicians and writers.

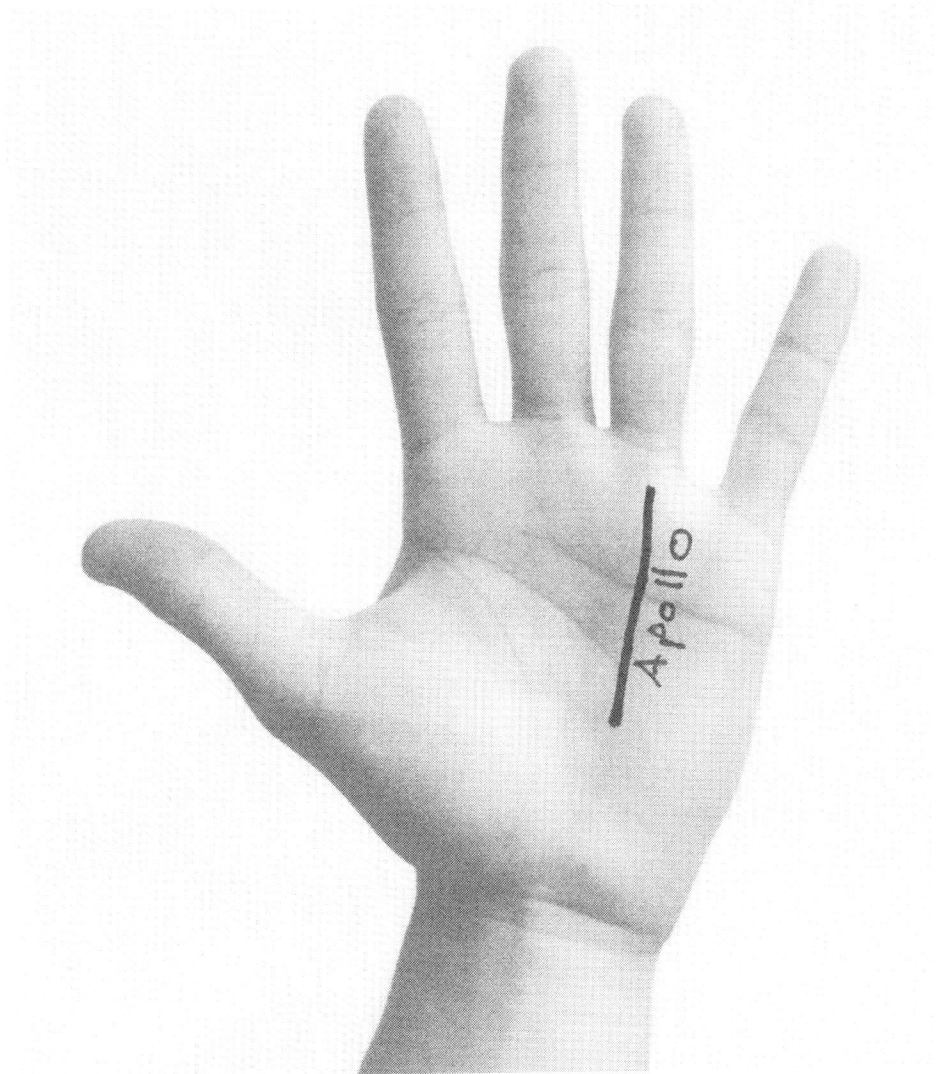

Apollo

Health Line

- When it appears, which is very rare, the Line of Health (also known as the Line of Mercury) moves from the Life Line toward the Mount of Mercury (the little finger).
- Typically, the appearance of this line indicates a strong physical constitution and health. Breaks or islands in the line may indicate problems with health.

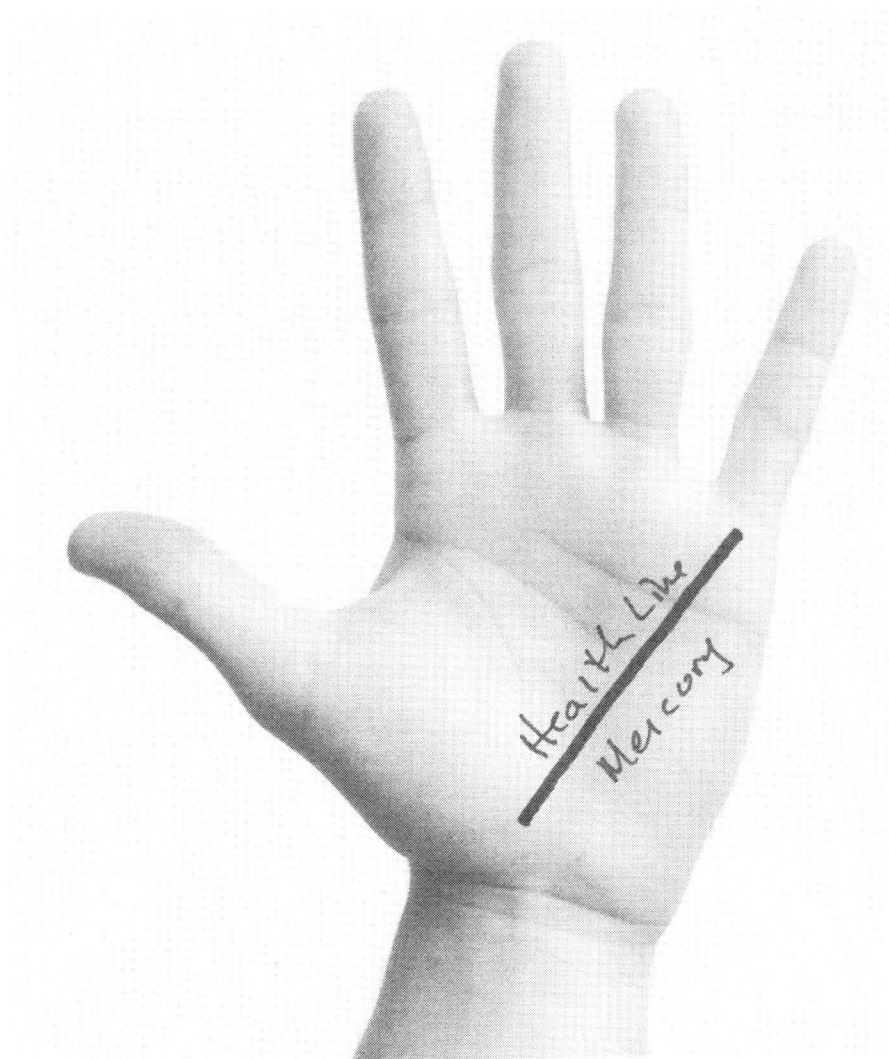

Health Line
Mercury

Girdle of Venus Line

- The Girdle of Venus looks like a second heart line, located between the heart line and top of palm. It may start and end at the top of the palm and curve downwards toward, but not touching, the Heart Line.
- It is found on only about 10% of clients, reinforces the heart line. It shows strong altruism, generosity, compassion. Can also indicate strong sexual responsiveness.

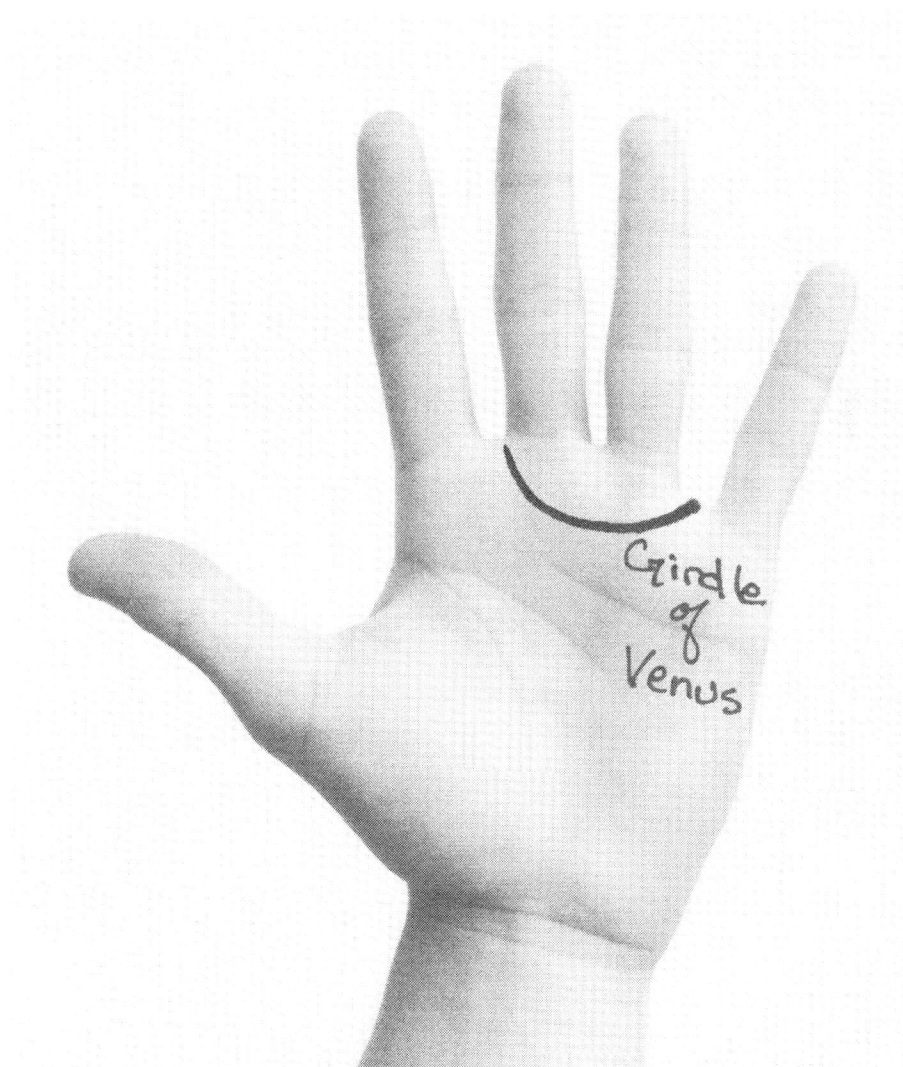

Girdle
of
Venus

Intuition Line

- The Intuition Line (also known as the Line of Uranus) is on the Luna Mount toward the Mercury Mount (the base of the little finger).
- Very rare. But, when present, it indicates powerful intuition. Most often found on clairvoyants, mediums and healers.
- Like other lines, this line can change and develop based on life changes, and efforts to develop intuitive skills can lead to development or strengthening of this line.

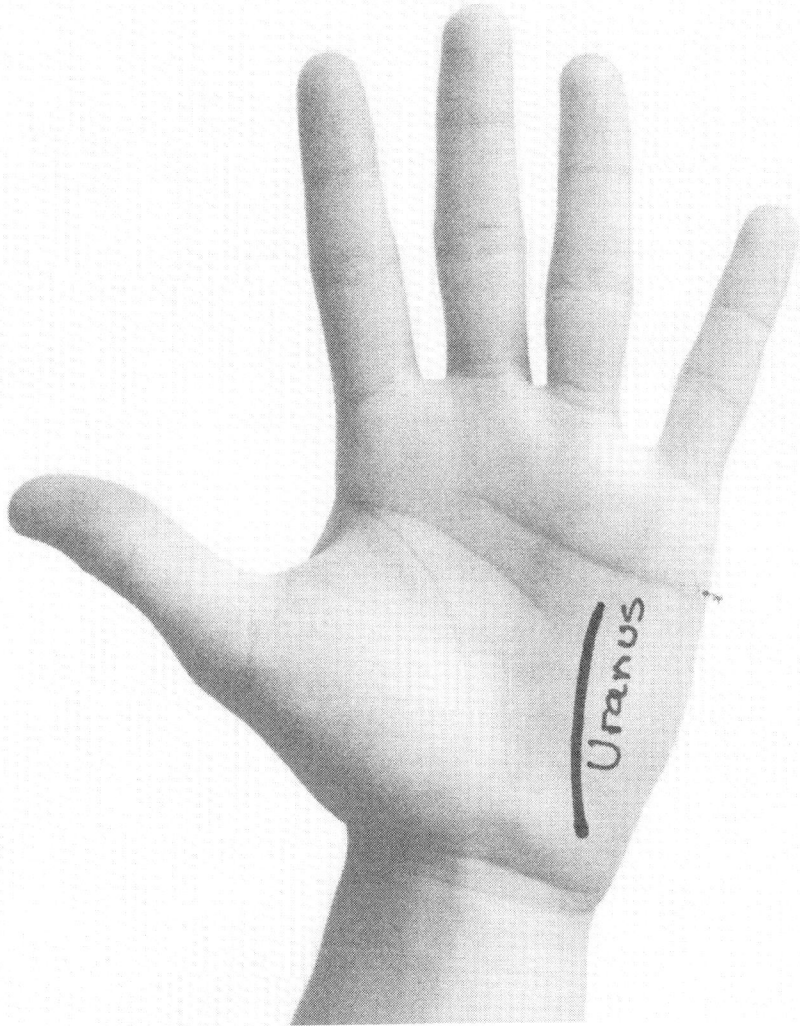

Travel Lines

- Rarely present, travel lines are small horizontal lines on the outer edge of the palm, along the Mounts of Luna and Mars and below the Heart Line.
- Each line represents an important trip. Not all travels are shown.
- The lines are in sequential order from bottom to top and the most important trips are longer and deeper lines

Union Lines

- Small horizontal lines representing strong unions, marriages, or other personal partnerships.
- The lines are in sequential order from bottom to top and represent only the most important relationships that were unions of some kind.
- The longer and deeper the lines, the stronger the union.

Children Lines

- There is lack of agreement on these lines. But, generally they appear as <u>tiny</u> horizontal lines below the Union Lines

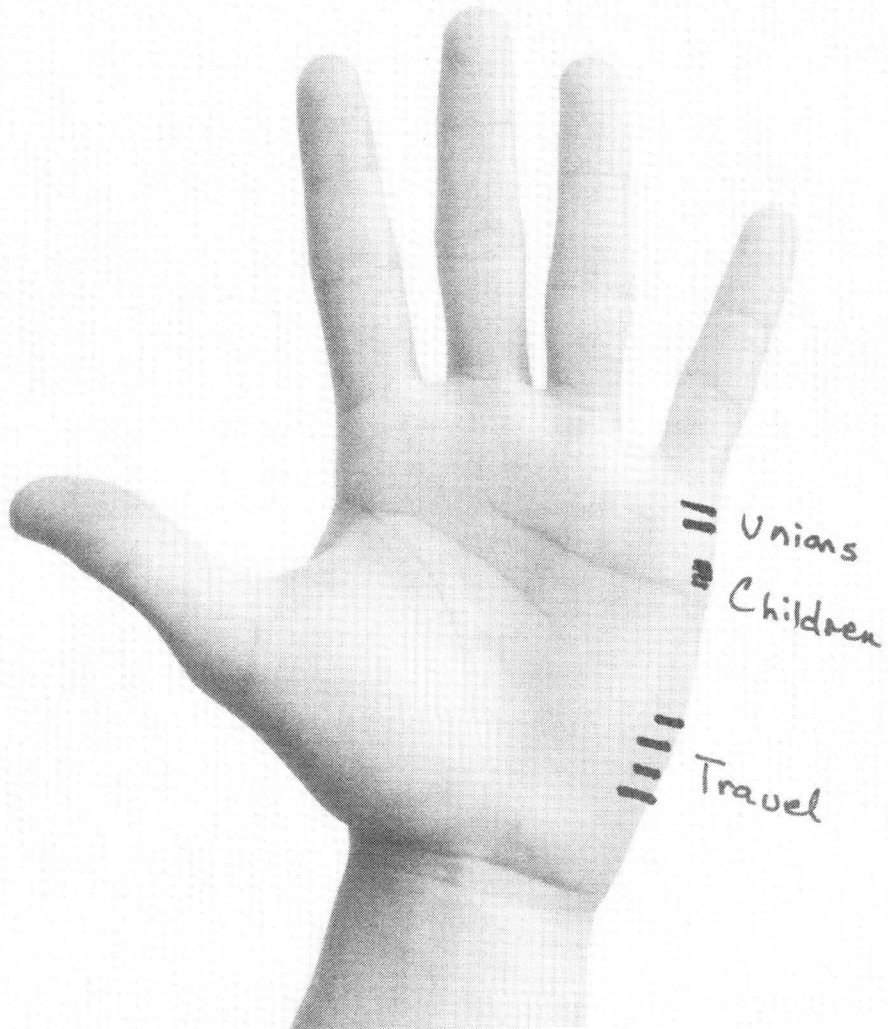

Unions

Children

Travel

Rascettes

- The Rascettes may be viewed as bracelets on the underside of the wrist.
- If strong and unbroken, each line indicates several decades of good health.

Lines of Influence

- Lines of Influence run parallel to the vertical lines of Life, Fate, and Capability.
- They strengthen these lines, when they appear. They may also repair the portion of line that they parallel, if that line has breaks, islands, or chains.

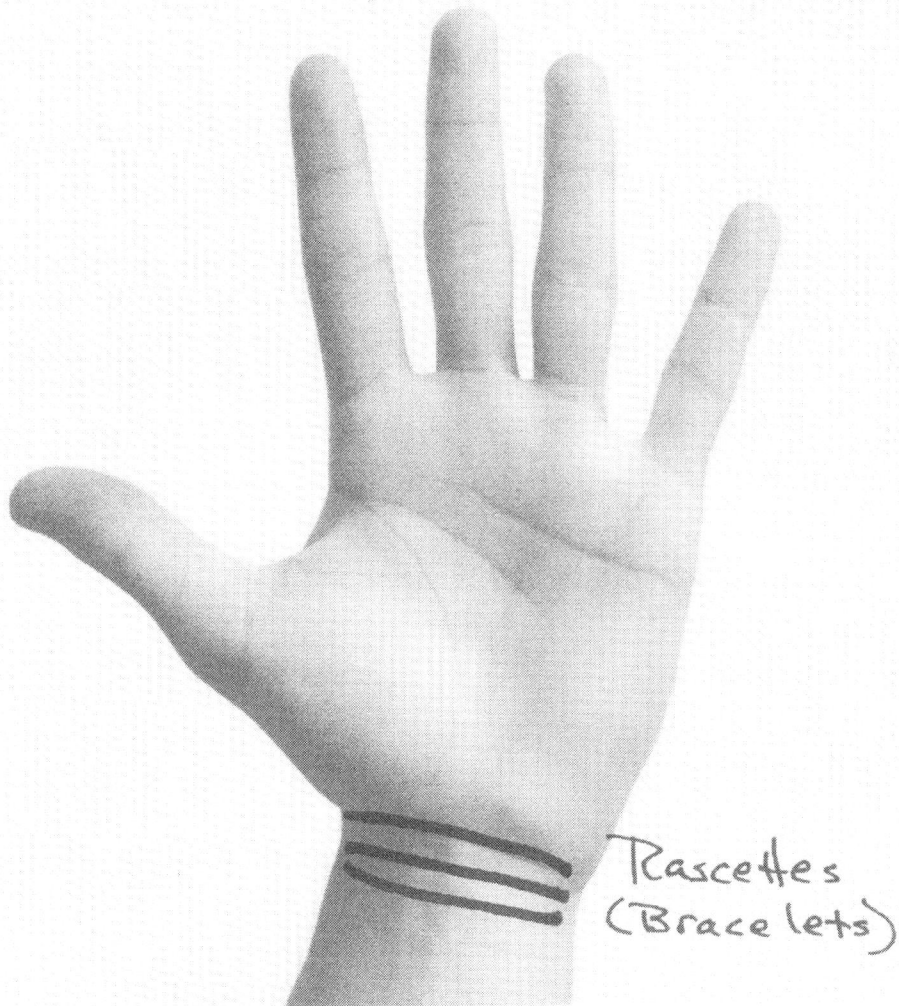

Rascettes
(Bracelets)

Time

Most of the time lines were developed decades ago, when lives were much shorter. They are not exact and only indicative of general time passage, so it is not possible to precisely know time of any event.

To accommodate the change in life lengths, consider the length of a line to indicate potential life and divide into segments. Where a viable vital life potential used to be about 75 years and a common vital career potential used to be about 40 years, these life and career periods have increased to 100 years and 55 years, respectively.

Also, lines change, so predictions for the long term are never valid. Only trends are possible to discuss, knowing that an informed person may then take steps to change and/or heal their lines.

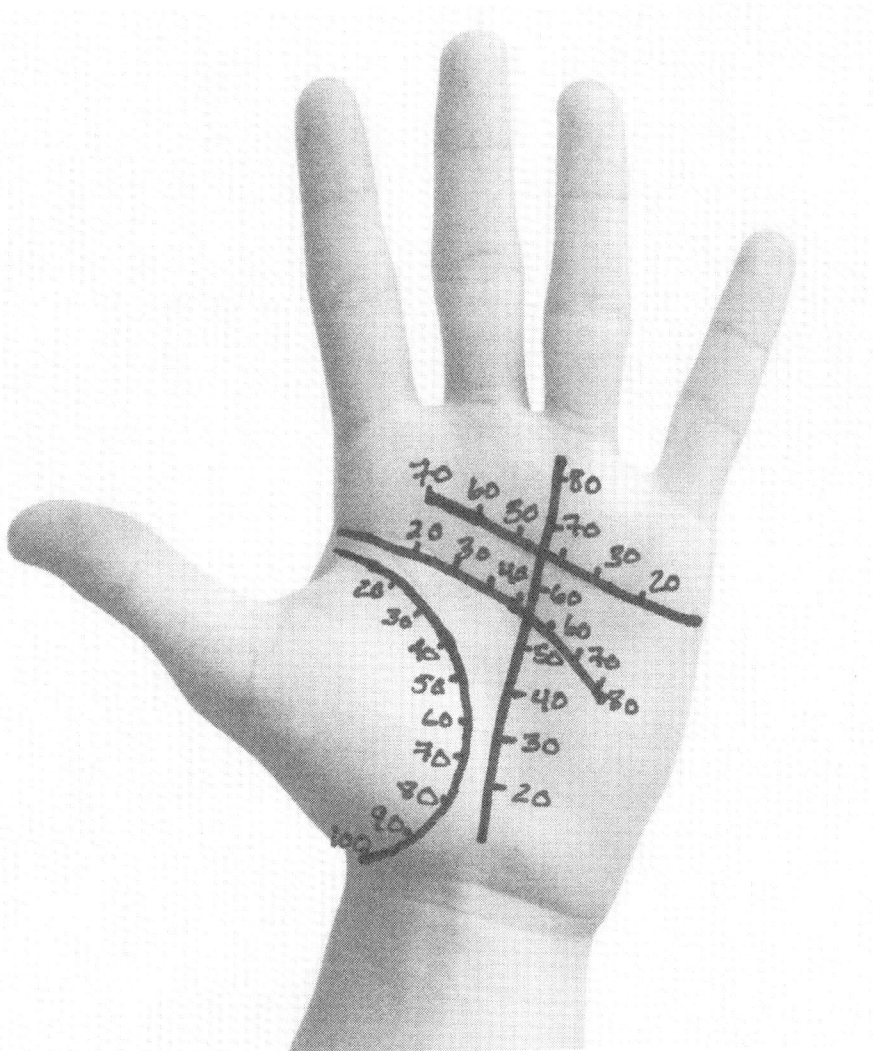

Marks

Marks on Lines, Palm Mounts and Finger Phlanges can either weaken or strength these items, as discussed below:

Lines of Influence or Sister Lines

Parallel lines to major lines, that strengthen the those lines. If the major line is broken, a parallel sister line the risk of the break is lessened or resolved.

Line with
Parallel
Lines of Influence

Lines that have Perpendicular Lines cutting across them

These small lines weakens the lines they cross.

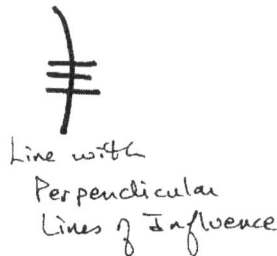

Line with
Perpendicular
Lines of Influence

Lines that are Broken

The end of something...unless mended by a square of parallel line of influence.

Broken
Line

A Square on a Line

If a line is broken or weak in parts, a square may exist like a bandaid to heal the line.

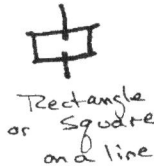

Rectangle
or Square
on a line

Lines that have segments that are Chained or are entirely Chained

A significantly weakened line.

Chained
line

Fork at the end of a Line

A two-pronged fork gives greater power to the line, as it indicates balance and flexibility in the line.

Fork end
on Line

Tassle at the end of a Line

A Tassle at the end of a line weakens the line and dissipates the energy of the line. This is the opposite of the two-pronged fork, above, which strengthens a line.

Tassle end
on Line

Lines with Ascending Branches or Descending Branches

Ascending Branches strengthen a line. Descending Branches weaken a line.

Branches
on Line

Lines with Islands

Islands show areas and times of weakness.

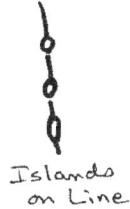

Islands
on Line

Lines with Spots

Spots, like Islands, are areas and times of weakness. Given their precision, they may indicate a specific event, rather than a general time and area of weakness.

Dotted
Line

Lines that have Wavy Segments

Waves weak the power of a line.

Wavy
Lines

Lines with fine and small capillary lines

Capillary lines weaken a line, much like a chained line is weakened.

Mounts covered with many fine lines of no color

Indicates weakness.

A Square or Circle on a Mount or Phalange

A healing, preserving, or strengthening mark, considered a gift of Spiritual favor.

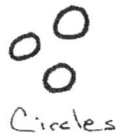

Circles

Stars or Crosses on a Mount or Phalange

An enhancing mark – like "star-crossed".

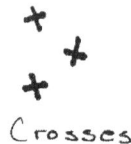

Stars   Crosses

Vertical lines on a Mount or Phalange

A very strengthening mark.

Verticals

Triangles between lines

May bridge the lines, something similar to the Square.

Triangles

Triangles on Mounts or Phalanges

A strengthening mark.

Horizontal lines on a Mount or Phalange

A very weakening mark.

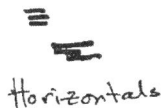

Horizontals

Grills on a Mount or Phalange

Hold in aspects and accentuates them, creating problems, like prison bars.

# #
# #

Grills

4

PRINTING THE PALM

<u>Printing the Palm for Historic Record:</u>

Obtain a rubber roller specialized for spreading printing ink – about 4 inches long.

Obtain a base for spreading the water-soluble black printing ink (can be smooth plastic or glass for using the roller to make a thin layer of ink.

Obtain soft art paper or newsprint. Not too still or smooth, as it needs to absorb the ink and bend into the crevices.

A tube of black water-base printing ink (the kind used to make block printing images – available at art stores).

Obtain a layer of foam rubber, such as a foam knelling pad for gardening, or something comparable which is not too soft, upon which to put the paper.

<u>Steps:</u>

1. Spread ink in a thin layer on the smooth surface with the roller, large enough for the entire palm and fingers.
2. Carefully ink the hand by lightly pressing on the inked surface, to have just enough to lightly cover the surface...not heavily inked, as that will hide the lines. Practice this and the next step often to be able to get good prints.
3. Place the paper on the foam surface and have the client put their inked hand on the paper in whatever is their natural way to hold their hand (with fingers spread or closed, as what they feel comfortable to do).
4. Press down on the client's hand, applying pressure to all parts and pushing gentle into foam to get a good print of most of the hand surface and fingers.
5. Have the client sign (signature) and date the print for your records.
6. This will enable the hand to be evaluated over time, as the hand and all its lines and marks changes. If you are a healer working with the client, it will be an interesting to monitor a baseline print with others printed later, for example...others taken once yearly...to see if certain lines and marks are improved or otherwise changed.

Note other features (such as mounts, flexibility and color), which will not be as obvious on the print. Now, with digital photography so readily available on telephones and notebooks, pictures can readily be taken to add to the printed record.

5

REFERENCES

(In order of their value to me as a palmist):

1. Language of the Hand: The Classic of Palmistry, by Cheiro, 1964.
2. The Benham Book of Palmistry, by Wm. G. Benham, 1988.
3. Secrets of the Palm by Darlene Hansen, 1985.
4. The Palmistry Workbook by Nathaniel Altman, 1984.

6

STANDARD WORKSHEET
FOR YOUR OBSERVATIONS

Worksheet for each Reading:

Name of Client:

Date:

Location:

General Observations from Comparing the Two Hands (Color, Texture, Flexibility, Differences between the Two Hands:

Size of Dominant Hand:

Shape of Dominant Hand:

Shape and Length of Fingers on Dominant Hand

Relative Length of Fingers with Each Other:

Angle of Thumb and Location of Where it Sits on Hand:

Prominent Mounts on Dominant Hand:

Overall Color and Texture of Dominant Hand:

Overall Depth and Color of Main Lines:

Overall Hand and Finger Flexibility:

Thumb Flexibility and Location:

Overall View of the Hand's Lines and Marks:

Overall View of the Hand's Smooth or Fine Lined Appearance:

Life Line:

Head Line:

Heart Line:

Fate Line:

Health Line:

Intuition Line:

Capability Line:

Union Lines:

Children Lines:

Travel Lines:

Rascettes:

Girdle of Venus:

Lines of Influence and Locations:

Marks and Locations on the Lines:

ACKNOWLEDGMENTS

Thank you to all my teachers and clients over the past forty years of my palm reading experiences. I have learned from each of you.

ABOUT THE AUTHOR

Sandra Cointreau is a professional civil engineer who has worked on environmental and waste management issues in over 60 developing countries in every region of the world. Over the more than 40 years of her travel for work, she has been fortunate to meet and observe the methods of many palm readers. In parallel, throughout her life, she has actively pursued a wide range of meditation, metaphysical and intuitive skills, including energy healing, positive manifestation, and telepathy. She has used her combined skills in research, analysis, and intuition to develop this clear and simple format for palm reading. She hopes this book will enrich and bless your life and bring many affirming palm reading experiences between you and your clients.

19145029R00043

Printed in Great Britain
by Amazon